Threshold of Resistance: Temple of Hope

Chelsea Dawn

BookLeaf Publishing

India | USA | UK

Presentation by *BookLeaf Publishing*

Web: www.bookleafpub.com

E-mail: info@bookleafpub.com

ISBN: 9789357444033

First edition 2022

I Travel Here

I travel here
Between the "shoulds", "want-tos", and musts,
Navigating the moments
moment to moment.

Switching lanes,
A caravan of intentions,
My Attention split between what surrounds me
and what I see within the windshield cinema of
my mind.

My body and mind drive on an acquired autopilot:
well-synced machinery and ancient coding,
while

My heart is a quiet passenger;
until

I pull over in a deserted lot.

Wild weeds thriving,
Silence for birdsong,
Stillness of Self,

Untamed Time.

I stretch the breath back into my body
and let life fill me again, and again,
heartbeat by heartbeat, lungful by lungful,
with what is more real than mind-stuff and
metaphor:

One moment; One mind; One heart,
in fantastic fractals of effort and surrender.

The destination remains
always, all-ways
Within.

I arrive safe, and serenely.

Dance

Unlock magic of marrow, and breath of blood;
ancient movement unremembered in the mind
yet echoing in memory of soul and breath of whole.

Follow the flow of living sorrow to the oceans of
tomorrow,
a current conundrum of flesh and mind,
a request spontaneous and consistent;
Heart's insistence to embody existence.

Victorious Love

Right and wrong
bow down before it
in sweet surrender,
Dissolving as salt crystals
into a sea of Truth:

Gladly, effortlessly, peacefully

Letting go of rigid form and familiar function,
Succumbing to fluidity.

Full immersion,
Separation slain with calm compassion,
and sight of vision.

Facades of power fall away
revealing
A temple matrix
of power and passion
Pure and true

Victorious
Love.

The Moment

Not hesitating or deliberating
when it's time to stop waiting.

Knowing when its time to stop
Knowing when its time to go;

Time to push and time to flow
Time to float and time to row;

Time to wonder and
Time to know.

Time to harvest, time to sow.

Anger

A storm slings sharp grains of sand, relentlessly
   exposing the forgotten, misunderstood, and
unprotected
      parts of my mind
         and the

unfinished prayers of my heart.

I am the storm
   I am the eye of the storm
      I am the wind
         I am the sand
            I am the sound
               I am sight and sensation;

And I am the storyteller
of each and every tender spot touched
   each and every callous caressed

numbness and apathy
   torn apart and
      polished with salt.

Mourning Death of Dignity

Letting go of could-have beens;
All regrets and sorrows on the mend.

Sea-ing

Turn my earth eyes inward,
so my mind's eye may look out,
and I may have Spirit vision.

Sometimes I Forget

My life is not a performance.
I do not owe the images anything.

I won't sell my peace to something smaller than my
Self.

Declaration

In defiance of false advertisements,
and programs I've purchased with my perception,

I choose to notice deception,

direct inception,

and summon protection of

Sovereign Discernment.

Meditation

Minding my mind's chatter:

a goal that serves my soul,
a practice that serves purpose;

Guide thoughts aside to make way for silence and
sensation.

Coping Mechanism

My self-doubt and perfectionism promise drama
and control;
deliver disappointment;
and cost consciousness.

Teasing Out Inner Tension

I pray that this emptiness becomes comfortable;
That I may release confusion and aimless awareness
And allow rejuvenation and joyful reflection.

While I wish for feeling different, I wish to be content
with what is,
and at peace with relentless wishing.
Ironic.

Often wishing, wanting, resisting what is,
What I desire most in the marrow of my bones
Is the comfort of a moment
Unmarred by assessment and comparison.

Thieves of joy, sowers of dissatisfaction,
Plundering abundance;
Tools out of context,
Misused, mismanaged, misunderstood.

And I know, though I forget,
Only in surrendering to the situation of this moment,
May I untangle taut thoughts and breathe again,
In freedom of movement
Forward.

I Am

Okay

I can be content with what is.

I am strong, I am tolerant.

I am aware of my wants and needs.

I am in dialogue with my body and mind, soul and
spirit.

I trust myself.

I trust the story.

I alchemize the unsavory to sweetness.

I reassess fairly, justly, and compassionately,

I rest, I exist.

I can be content with This.

Time =/= Money

Create space for emptiness and clarity;
Do not fill the moments automatically.

Sensation of time is not for quantification or
consumption,
But for craftiness of creation.

Love, As a Fire

Ablaze in a meadow,
Aflame in a forest.

A wood stove;
A candle upon an alter;
A reading lamp.

An eruption of the sun;
An emergence of inner Earth;
A torch of truth.

Combustion engines,
Pyrotechnics, detonations,
Wildfire of infatuation.

Warmth and comfort;
Sustenance and safety.

Singing circles, sweat lodge;
Ancient Fire of the Heart,
Sparks reflecting eternal stars

Paradox

This is an experiment.

The doing, the not doing;
The being, the becoming.

Where I go, and what I leave behind.
Who I meet, and who I miss.
What I say and what I mean;
How I feel and how I act.

Making tradeoffs, making choices;

Letting go, holding on;
Desire and detachment.
Turning in and tuning out,
Reaching down and
Rising up.

Centering expansion,
Reflections informing;
Singing and silence,
Stillness and Dance.

Eternal, Ephemeral:
The Divine mirrored by the Mundane.

Observations

Witnessing love's creation,
destruction and reorganization;

unraveling
no longer mattering
back to patterning.

There Is Mystery

There is a mystery;

and

a mysterious desire among humankind

to understand

something else.

Love Is

Back to back on a yoga mat
Chanting sanksrit.
Gently and persistently guiding our minds to that
present moment,
He and I,
Tending to our togetherness.

Grief Is Love

Make room for wounds
          and grief that blooms
               into

gratitude.

Cake

Whoever made the claim
that we ought not
have our cake and eat it too

Must not know cake-making
and cake-eating:
Must not know cake.

They must have forgotten that celebrations come
as often as wished, inspired, and recognized,

And that a cake uneaten is not a cake, merely an
exercise in baking.

Have your cake and eat it too,
And share it.